Purple Carnations

Aanya Biswas

BookLeaf Publishing
India | USA | UK

Presentation by *BookLeaf Publishing*

Web: www.bookleafpub.com

E-mail: info@bookleafpub.com

ISBN: 9789363314764

First edition 2024

To my aunt,
For being both my sword and shield

Preface

Purple carnations symbolise unpredictability and capriciousness.

That is exactly what life is like. It's unpredictable. You never know the exact time when a flower might bloom or when a flower might wilt and die. You never know when a volcano might burst or when a tsunami can sweep over the land. You never know when an earthquake might take place. You never know how long wounds take to heal.

And that's the thing with humans.

Most of them have made it their mission to figure out the logistics and the workings of everything in the world.

Even the human brain.

But different people think and perceive different things in their own way. No amount of knowledge or years spent studying can solve how the human mind functions.

Science and logic can't be applied to anything and everything.

Sometimes all you need is a book, a little ink, and a bunch of words.

Words can either break a person or could rip them apart. Sometimes, make it look like child's play.

Or they could heal a person.

And I can't control how you feel. No one can.

But I just hope that they make you feel something. Anything. Anger. Frustration. Hope. Joy. Peace.
Anything.

—Aanya

Table of contents

59. I'm sorry
60. Sayonara
61. Ragdoll
62. Lightning
63. I saw you in the dark
64. Sink
65. One day
66. All lies
67. Someone once said
68. The painting
69. Love is war
70. Traffic lights
71. Something better left unsaid
72. Insane
73. All wrong
74. Other than me
75. The town of peace
76. When will the world stop turning?
77. Dead meadow's arc
78. Candlelight
79. Stumble
80. Flashback
81. Same page
82. Grapevine
83. Dove of death
84. When the movie ends
85. Fury
86. Christmas girl
87. The creature in disguise
88. Changing seasons
89. Hit by a train
90. Caged
91. The rare

Pathways

This river of red
Flowing so freely in my veins
The star of the north
That has guided me through the twisted lanes

The intensity and pain of the stars
That paints the infinite skies
The solicity of the moon
That has seen the neverending lies

This ruin of rubble and stone
That lies helplessly tumbled in the mud
The souls that lurk in the dark
Their destinies forever tainted with blood

This heart, both alive and dead
Wounded and shall never heal
The beauty of clockwork
That never reveals the fake or real

Each puzzle piece, shattered and broken
That painted everything around blue
This garden of cosmos and valley of stars
That has somehow led me to you.

The artist

Fall in love with darkness
And never again, will you find the light
Fall in love with a weapon
And you'll be stuck in a never-ending fight
Fall in love with the truth
And you shall never find the lie
But fall in love with an artist
And you shall never die.

Annabelle

Pretty doll, come haunt my dreams
Make me forget about my nightmares
For you're not even half as scary
Than my life story, it's beyond compare

Pretty doll, come loudly outscream
Every single one of my thoughts
Make me only hear you
So that I don't have to hear the whole other lot

Just infiltrate me with temporary fear
For the time being
For you're just child's play
From all the horrors I've been seeing.

Flame

The clouds are on fire
And the ashes are raining down
Everything feels suffocated
From the flame that is ringing about

But it's the people they say
Those who caused the chaos
Those who set the world on fire
Those who have lines crossed

Think again for once
Figure out why the tables have turned
Why is it someone thinks that
It's our fault, the world has burnt

Look at the sky for once
Then decide which lunatic
Thought that it was us playing with fire
And not the sky that was handed the matchstick.

The entertainer

If the ship is about to go underwater
I would not give it twice a thought and straight
away sink with you
Because I'd rather get suffocated by the water
Then not being the one you're next to

If the house was on fire
I'd let myself get swallowed by the flames
Because I'd rather burn my flesh and bone
Than live in the grieving kind of pain

If I could tell you one thing
I'd tell you not to let your good heart get in the
way
Of all your dreams and all your wishes, face the
nightmares too
And forever be underneath the hope of the sun's
ray

Forever will you always have my support
No matter what others say
Because you were always there with me
Even on all of my darkest days

Like the calming waves of the ocean
You would comfort me with your silence
You would take me in your arms
And make me forget about all the bad memories and violence

These memories I will take with me to the grave
I vow to never have them lost
You'd give everything without giving me anything at all
And it was one of your many gifts which gave free of cost

Laughing at this unfair world as you held me close
Pretending to be asleep when we were talking for hours on end
The one person who always had my back, and with it all my trust
With you, I never have to pretend

You made me believe in the world
And you made me believe in myself
Our song will always be a comfort
Whenever I am not feeling myself

These words have come to me so fast
It's like even they will not do enough justice
To how much you have always healed me
The one person who I have always trusted

You have told me it's okay to have battle scars
And it's okay to feel suffocated like you can't be free
I have too many words in my head but one thing I wanted to say is
I love you like the sunset loves the sea.

Heart Masquerade

This is a world where everyone walks around
with their heart in chains
Trying their best to keep it hidden from the view
Don't people ever get tired of the continuous
taste of lies on their tongues?
Their conscience is mocked as it is thrown into
the fire and barbequed

This world will forever be a masquerade
Where everyone hides their heart instead of
their faces
Keeping it at bay, hoping it will never escape its
freezing jail
Hypnotised into thinking all the words of the
heart are 'outscreamed' by the lie's embraces.

The grave

Awake the unawakened
And lead me into the tomb of the forgotten
The killer's moon has arrived
And the creatures will drag you to the bottom

Harm, not the innocent lives
Leave them untouched
But let me revive your soul
With the hands, you could have clutched

But let go, I did
I threw it into the deep depths
Stumbling over my wounds
Rather than the crooked steps

Your spirit looming over another
While I stand putting the flowers in front of the tomb
For I want you to loom over me instead
Over the incandescent moon

I'd built this over both nothing and everything
Like some lonely faded away shrine
Let me revive your soul
For that is the only thing that can revive mine

This neverending vast universe.

PART I

The moon

I told the skies that no one would see the true
me
Because reality has scared even the moon into
giving up
I told the stars only they would know my secret
But it's getting tiring to keep filling a
never-ending cup

I told the planets to not say a thing
Because one second I'm crescent and the next I
am gone
I told the comets that everything will be alright
But in this neverending vast universe, I myself
feel like I don't belong

They told me about the others
And I listened to everything through and
through
And they listened to me
As I told them about you.

PART II

The Planets

Tired of circling the sun
Just want to float off this orbit
I just want to feel my surrounding
Without the leisure and absorb it

This was the cruelty
I never wished to face
But it is an eternal reality
That no one can escape

The many phases I've seen
Of life itself
How many thunderstorms and sun's rays
Hitting my surface have I felt

But I'm stuck in a forever loop
That keeps on repeating
We might not have a body
With a heart that is beating

But nevertheless even though we don't have a
voice
That can't protect ourselves
We are broken all the same
And there is no one to cry for help.

PART III

The stars

Our efforts never satisfied anyone
No matter how bright, most will only see dots
The ones that glow in the sky
For how much none knows we fought

But now that hope is going
Uselessly tossed
No matter how bright
The light has us lost

But we too shatter like glass
Go off with a huge blast when we can't bear it anymore
Willing for the tide of darkness
To take us past the shore.

Globe

Someone rattled the globe
For everything is tipping down
The people, the plants, the animals
All floating off the ground

And landing into the unknown
Like every creature was destined to
Now I talk of you only to the stars
Hoping amidst the darkness that they would
recognise you.

Olive Tree

Took me to a garden and planted an olive tree
Next thing I knew, you were tearing it down
piece by piece

And on days when I feel like I can't be myself
I look at the dead branches, still somehow
crying for help

Now the flowers lay wilted and the leaves like
parchment
And darkness now fills up the space around the
roots, living there free of rent

No amount of water or sunlight can help heal
This dead tree, no longer able to feel

For its time had already come a long long time
ago
And every part of it has become an ally of the
dark, and sunlight its foe

And now look around and tell me what exactly
do you see
It is a garden filled with thousands of different
plants that started with that one olive tree

Though that tree haunts a past that has always bleeded
Now it's just a mere memory, for that one olive tree is now no longer needed.

Genie

Vanished into thin air
Three wishes left ungranted
The happiness of youth now uprooted
Now can no more be planted

Get back the golden chest
Someone threw so far away
Lacking my reason to live and with it my rest
All kept away at bay

Rewind the time again
And delete the past
I don't care if I fade
Because bonds are meant to last

And give a steady sword
That can pierce through anyone's heart
Let them for once know what it feels like
To have your conscience left scarred

But the lamp was shaken too hard
And now mere trust has turned rotten
And why are you mad now
When it was you who had forgotten.

Kaleidoscope

Forever will I live in the kaleidoscope
For the colours have me bewitched
But dried blood still stains the floor
And the wounds of it cannot be stitched

It's not the land that is damaged
But the people who created each and every
broken piece
Them who left this world scarred
But it was this that created such a masterpiece

Each and every piece has its worth
For each day a new pattern is made when
someone moves it
The emptiness it would cause
When someone takes the pieces and removes it

Because each shattered thing that lays upon this
splintered floor
Has helped in creating some messed up pattern
And each is a different mess but a unique one
Like the glorifying rings of Saturn.

Fall

So far apart from this vast sea
Nevertheless, you still somehow find ways to set
your auburn shades over it as you fall down

And it catches you and lets you float
For it knows the damage these falls have caused
you, and it refuses to be the reason you drown

And enough damage you have seen
So much that even the tides and the waves feel
sorry

And enough deafening noise have you heard
So much that the creatures of the deep also
worry

Forever will you have the reassurance
That there will always be someone to catch you
Someone who shows no mercy
And leaves others to die but you

Because the sea already knows the pain you have
experienced
And no matter which path of shattered dreams
the sea has to choose

None of them will do any justice to what horrors the sunset faced
For it has already seen everything and there is nothing left to prove.

Pages

A heart so long left silenced
Always torn apart
A million words left unsaid
That is bound to leave a mark

A story left unfinished
And pages now so arcane
It's like being in a picture-perfect photo
With a really broken frame

This book must've belonged to a witch
For these pages have been beshrewed upon
Each and every single word, a reminder
Of the past I've always wished begone

But few words will forever leave me enchanted
One of which I can escape never
And now that they have found me
They'll be bound to me forever.

Dagger

A crime has been committed
And no one knows whose hands are red
A heart helplessly lying on the floor
Now faded away and dead
The knife lies on the ground
Blood staining the whole floor
That was the last thing you gave to me
A dagger that will haunt me forevermore.

Wounded

After all this time
I still see you knocking on the door
Because you still want to know
What could've been the life you live no more

All that thunder was left hidden
And behind a carefully woven tapestry, you lived in silence
Like a dangerous dance of knives
You remained immune to the violence

Or at least that's what everyone thought
Because it was all they could ever see
A wish wholeheartedly fulfilled
And now set free

Seeing everything wounded around you
You looked at them too
But something you did not realise
That the one who was wounded the most was you.

The abyss

You jumped into the abyss
There you froze to death
But where is the fun in that
When you can experience me taking my last
breath?

And with your icy heart
You come around like a disease
And like a chain reaction
When I touch you, I too begin to freeze.

Ashes

I own an unsolvable maze
One that is called my heart
There hasn't been one time I didn't hit a dead
end
For I always end up returning to the start

And there was a time when
Joy was allowed some room
But now this mystery maze
Is shredded in nothing but gloom

The walls of it always stop the light
From ever seeping through
The blossoms growing there
Don't know the feeling of sunlight, not one clue

All I hope is that people will
Stop trying to make me whole
And stop thinking my heart as the leftovers of a
fire
Scattered throughout the floor, both ashes and
coal

Because these ashes will be the reminder
That not everything ever stays
And that is how even the leftovers of a fire
Have a role to play.

Echo

You escaped this land
But your presence never faltered
Not from their mind nor their soul

Your rhythm left the song
But your echoes
Are enough to make a person whole

Your wounds are so faint
But the scars somehow still hurt
For your sting is never going to leave

And you are not dead
But your presence
Still causes some people to grieve

For you might only be the echoes in a forgotten song
But that will not change the fact that the real rhythm is long gone.

Tempest

Threw me into the deepest depths
There grew a storm left long unkempt

These aphonic walls caving in, locking me with
these unheard thoughts and choices
The thrashing waves so loud it began, it drowns
out all the other noises

The waters rhythm, canorous and calm
About to burst like a ticking time bomb

Everything in here not having a care in the
world, leaving me be
The heartbeat of it so continuous and evergoing,
it has become a part of me

Its waves now the key to each emotion
Its walls no longer a cage, but a guard called the
ocean

Its shore where my conscience decides to roam
when things get too much
Its waters, cool under my palm, calming me
with just one touch

The stars always guiding me when the sea has
me lost
The surface always there to catch me when these
rough waters have me turned and tossed

The corals, crooked but beautiful, a reminder
that nothing is perfect
And watching the ocean catching the sunset's
auburn, a struggle worth it

These waters which belong to none, moving
independently and freely
It made me discover a tempest, that I never
knew was inside me

And it helped me unleash it to its fullest
potential and set it free
For each heartbeat of this vast ocean has finally
become a part of me

For now this dark unknown is where I belong
And no more does it drag me down
But imposters, if they come in
In this tempest, you shall drown

For you were the one that threw me in
Thinking I won't survive
But not only did I rise
With the ocean, now a part of me, I thrive.

Words left unsaid

Didn't you see her fight each nightmare?
Her voice as sound as the ocean but her eyes
livid
Yet you did nothing
But make those nightmares even more vivid

Didn't you hear her scream?
Among this endless silence
Yet you did nothing but make it worse
Forcing her to remain quiet within this violence

Didn’t you see her with the sword?
As she fought and fought
And yet you left her on the battlefield, alone
Without a single thought
Without a single thought.

Raven and Dove

You think these trees will grow on this
droughted land
No amount of convincing will make you
understand
You think that nothing leaves a mark
You think that these flowers will be able to
bloom in the dark
Either you are too lost in your own dream
For your eyes are never open to the dark but only
the sunbeam
And you've never felt the dark and dim
A stirring storm, growing more chaotic within
For you, only the doves can come this high
Then why do I still see the ravens circling the
sky?

Broken dreams

Each and every drop of ink
Wasted away on this holy grave of words
Each and every crucial thought
That found a home here, silent but can still be heard

Each and every hopeless wish
Crashed with the shooting star
Each and every stubborn path
Never near neither far

Each and every vivid dream
So clear it could be painted out
Each and every rainforest
Now facing a severe drought

Each and every diamond
That found itself stuck in the rough
Each and every grain of sand
That powered its way through both the pleasant and tough

Each and every broken canvas
With a paintbrush now thrown away
Each and every endless night
Never reaching a pleasant day

Each and every wilted flower
That was forced to perish in the dark
Each and every child of flame
Harmed by its own spark

And forever will this conscience of mine
Keep stumbling upon the same loophole
For a part of me has drifted away
And with it, it has taken my soul.

Blood

The sky is turning red
The hues seem to disappear
I'm blinded by pitch black
With you no longer here

Your echoes like a siren
Never leaving me
Your shadows all around
Going to a new degree

Dancing in the stardust
Of my very own shot-down star
Shattered dreams, no more permanent
Hour after hour

You're covered in ink
On every single page
Etched permanently in the stone
Hurtling in the deep's rage

You're here on the land
The skies and everywhere
Each symphony your rhythm
And no one seems to care

I thought you'd be the waters
But now I'm wild in the flood
All that stain's my canvas now
Is blood, blood and blood.

The tremor

This ground shakes beneath my feet
And the mountains are tumbling
The tsunamis consumed each and every island
underwater
And the trees and plants are crumbling

Fallen at the feet of god
Left for them to decide its fate
And no matter how long they spend running
away
Time shall never wait

And within the snap of the fingers
Within the blink of an eye
Every single thing shall disappear
From the ground to the sky

And the lord shall spare none
For it shows no mercy
It ties your fate in chains
And so they'll never be set free.

The nook

Went into the nook and found a friend
One who holds my hand, whenever I hit a dead end

It pulls me out of these shallow holes with a steady rope
It extinguishes my fire and with it all my hope

It takes all my ashes and throws them in the way
It becomes my personal haunted house, scaring me night and day

It's on every single page and the chapters never end
It is you darkness, I am talking about my friend

But I wish I could rewind, and leave you there in the nook
Maybe then I can take back every single hour that you took

Chaos is for eternity but only in darkness have I grown
Because till my dying breath will you haunt me for in darkness I was sown.

Everything

You were my sea
But look how I've drowned
You were my skies
But look how my feet have fallen on the ground

You were my melodies
But the guitar is now split in half
You were my voice
But you've consumed each and every laugh

You were my flame
But look how I've burnt
You were my escape
But look how the tables have turned

You were my north star
But now I have a starless sky
You were my wings
But now I struggle to fly

You were my sea, skies and land
You were my everything
And I got consumed by you so much
That my stardust faded away into nothing.

Cage

These walls I've built to protect myself
Are turning into a cage
These words I wrote to assure myself
I won't let history repeat itself on each page

These whispers that keep on hypnotising me
Are turning into the loudest of screams
These wishes I thought could come true
someday
Are turning into worst of my dreams

These melodies that once used to comfort me
Have now become a dangerous siren's song
These bars that I can never escape
Is the only place they say, I belong.

Burn

You thought that I burned
But rather you breathed fire into me
A fire that won't burn out
But a fire that will spread wildly

And within the palm of hand
Will I hold this flame
For my heart
Is no more in your claim

And if you shall
Come too close and turn
With the fire you ignited within me
You will burn.

Forever

The beat of this guitar is the only thing
That understands the beat of my heart
And these pages are the only thing that truly
know
What it feels like to be torn apart

And these lyrics are the only things
That can truly feel each word
These walls are the only thing
That comfort me when my music goes unheard

Chords are the only thing
That understand what it feels like to be pulled
on the chords of your soul
What it feels to be played
Never satisfied and never quite whole

These guitar strings are the only thing
That not only see, but feel the rhythm of my
emotion
Like a tide that comes and goes
Bearing it like the ocean

And it never leaves me aside
Rather it plunges deeper into my soul
For it's something that will forever be stitched
into me
Forever making me whole

No matter all the endless loopholes
We shall part never
People come and go
But this? This is forever.

Forever Part II

Forever was an illusion
It was made of broken promises and shattered things
Forever was an illusion
Fragile and bound with nothing but mere rings

Forever, they say is made of gold
But its crust is made of all but brass
Forever, they say is made of imperial metal
Then why does it shatter like glass

Whispers saying that when the world is black and white
Forever makes you see the carmine and aquamarine
Forever refuses to show itself on a plain surface
It's impossible to vision it all on nothing but a screen

Forever, it's a dangerous thing
It's a dream that can't come true
But nevertheless, it doesn't matter
For I would dream of forever for you.

Wizard

All ask,
How do I have so much magic in my eyes?
It was all because of a wizard
Who enchanted me with all their lies

Forever shall I be cast under your spell
Because I never want to let go of this trance
For I never want to let go of the possibility
That even the sun and moon can dance.
Or are people just too blinded by the sun's light
to see it?

Spirit

How crazy it is
That you escaped this house
And you escaped this dream
You cast on a spell of
'What was' now 'what would seem'

But you never really escaped these pages
Nor did you the mind
You only escaped your physical self
From this daily grind

But I can still feel your spirit
Lurking around each door
Never really leaving
Always coming back for more

And I can still hear your whispers
Late at night
I can still see your silhouette
Even when to others, you are out of sight

Whether the sun is there
And whether it is not
You never escaped this land
You never escaped a single thought

Sometimes when I forget about you
You reappear
Like the stars in the sky
You are always here.

Bleed

If the people wrecked the world
Like the wreckage in their hearts
This world would be in a billion shambles
Ripped, stabbed and torn apart

Its core smashed and thrown
With a beating heart it did not need
But if they wrecked the world
Like the heart, it would bleed and bleed.

Your spirit

These embers of this flame are about to tire
Nevertheless, set this world on fire

In every dream, I see your ghoul
Slowly and steadily seeping into my soul

No matter which crossroad I tread
Everywhere this spirit of yours wants me dead

It wants to savour the feel of my blood on its hands
Haunt my conscience and its lands

But your touch, no matter how rough brings me comfort
The wounds distract me from the real cause of the hurt

And whenever it enters my heart's terrain
It brings nothing but excruciating pain

But I don't care, I like the way it stings
At least then I don't have to pay attention to the other things

Like a broken heart and the hurricane in my mind
I'm walking into your ditch for I have gone blind

Take my heart, please take it away
It is yours to keep, yours to haunt night and day

So I'd willingly give you my heart
Take it and tear it apart.

Fake

My voice is such a melody
Then why do I hide from the crowd
The horrors all so silent
No matter how loud

The tsunamis in my eyes
In my head, each earthquake
I've been paralysed
For I got bitten by a snake

All the chapters people turned
All the plot twists I saw
The words suited to kill
Like that of a lion's maw

Why are the blossoms left to wilt
Out there in the dark
They don't have a clue
For the minds got swallowed up by a shark

Why so silent all of a sudden?
Can't see all that I despise
But of course you're going to blame it
On the bat's wings that keep flapping in front of
your eyes

Call me young
And call me free

But I can no longer function
With all these wounds on my body

Call me responsible
And call me aware
But the very girl you relied on
Is now getting mauled by a bear.

Wildfire

You're etched in my heart
You're in my flesh and bone
Your name up in the skies
And also set in stone

Never seeming to flicker
Your bulb's glow, never dying
But my filaments broken
Dead over there, just lying

No one there to pick it up
But no strength have I left
So I'm staring at it, it's staring back at me
Throwing away the dignity, I long kept

You're everything I see
Flowing through my veins
You're the wildfire I dreamt of
Coming down like the rain.

The one

I thought you were the embers
I thought you were moon
I thought you were the magic wand
That would wave away this gloom
I thought you were the torch
I thought you were the North star
I thought that from a distance
I could know whether you were near or far
I thought you were the gold
I thought you were the laugh
I thought that suffocation
Would stitch back both my halves
I thought you were the diamond
Waiting in the rough
I thought all these boxes and memories were thrown
With all the other stuff
I thought you were the lightbulb
I thought you were the sun
I thought you were everything to me
I thought you'd be the one.

Crash

This life is like a car
And I'm in the driver's seat
Trying to take myself somewhere
As I can't travel on my feet

I'm going past the limit
Going as fast as I can
The whole world says 'Slow down, will you?'
And I swear I'm trying, I am

But right now my mind is haywire
For I don't care where I go
I just hope I don't end with the same chaos
I have long come to know

But chaos is my friend
For it always tags along
Following me like the echoes
In a never-ending song

Oh lord, here comes chaos
I'm gonna speed up a little bit
Hopefully it won't catch up
And I won't get hit

I've taken a wrong turn
Now I have no idea where the hell I'm going

Blame the car! Not me
For not knowing

Stop the car, stop the car
It doesn't seem to stop
Now I think I sped too much
That it doesn't seem to care if I crash or not

BOOM goes my car
I look at my wounds and wince
Chaos has caught up to me
And I've been scarred ever since.

Someone I used to know

Everywhere I look I see you
You're pierced in my heart
You've been a backward marathon I want to run
From the end to the start

They all state out
You're gonna suffocate
And all the noise is been blocked out
For everything is all but a blank slate

You're here and you're there
Maybe you've taken up a little too of my space
I'm running and running with you
But we're running away from this race

All I'm scared about is
I'll run so much that my lungs will cease to work
And instead you'll start to run away from me
But in my mind and heart you'll still lurk

And you'll be all but the past
One of the many who decided to go
For you'll slowly turn into a memory
Of someone I used to know.

Limbo

For long in this sand
I have been sifting
My eyes trying to blink away the sleep
Slowly, I am drifting

Into a limbo
I won't be able to come out
But maybe this peace
Is just what will water my drought

Maybe a little meditation
Is all I really need
From stopping my flesh and mind
From its constant bleed

Forever will I always
Be in the trance
With the mind and heart constantly
Stuck in a dangerous dance.

Corpse

Not yet a coma patient
But mind always fast asleep
Never quite awake
Too shut down to take a leap

But somehow not part of this world
Gone mentally
I may as well have bashed myself against the
wall
And said it was done accidentally

Not yet a disaster
But my head is an earthquake
Never stops trembling
Always seems to shake

Not yet shut down
But my heart is a buffered screen
Always seems to be loading
A gone case machine

Not yet a corpse
Laying in the moonlight
Buried within roses
Gloomy in sight

But somehow still dead
Buried in the ground

But no one seems to care at all
And I shall too never be found

Take away this pain
I no longer want to keep
But it won't go away
For it's in a little too deep

Not yet a corpse
At least that is what they said
But a person can be buried, can't they?
For a part of them is already dead.

Pirate's ship

I think I have been placed
Inside a pirate's ship
I don't know who to trust here
If I go stumbling off the tip

Everyone else here
Knows exactly what to do
But me? I don't even know why I'm here
This reality doesn't seem to be true

Trying to escape this ship
I think I need a map
I'll try my best not to mess things up
I'll stay away from every possible mishap

But where is this so-called map
Everytime time I look for it a new threat is yet to come
Legend says it's in a hidden closet
Placed next to the stale rum

The clues never seem to come along
I think I have run out of luck
I'll never be able to escape without the map
Forever in this ship I am stuck.

Bewitched

I saw something lurking in the shadows
Something I've never seen before
I heard it knocking on my heart
I heard it knocking on my door

But for the first time ever
I wanted to let it in
I wanted to unleash this creature
That found a home in me within

It's scary how I want this
Maybe a little too much
I think I see myself bewitched
With just a single touch

The way you pull me in
Whenever I pretend to go
The way you laugh with me
Whenever I tiptoe

Whenever I tiptoe over reality
For with you I'm forever stuck in a dream
All I'll ever be scared about is
Things are the way they actually seem

You make feel like maybe
This journey I can survive
Not only did you bring back from the dead
But you made me feel alive.

The words my mom could never say

You said you'd wipe away these tears
Whenever I wanted to cry
You did nothing but haunt my dreams
And stitch me into a lie

We were just a broken promise
Bound together by a ring
You must have felt nothing at all
While I was feeling everything

The places you promised you'd take me
The different oceans and cruises
But all you ever took me to
Was the endless ride of broken bones and
bruises

You crowned me as your queen
On a land only you could rule
You planted fake flowers in the garden
Thinking I was a fool

The pain would numb me at first
But through these cracks, slowly it started to
seep
You wounded me with your words
And it all cut so deep

These pages were the only thing
Left for me of comfort
Other than I sat there wallowing
In this endless hurt

These walls, they saw everything
The floor caught my tears
This stupid ring on my hand
Unleashed my greatest of fears

It stuck me in a marathon
One big endless race
But it was you I was running from
And this suffocating haze

You took away my dignity
You took away my time
You took away each hour
Without giving back a dime

I feel a little empty
You never understood
You were too much of a coward to try
But it was because you didn't have it in you, you never could

Convinced everyone
Of some magical fake fantasy
Stuck me in a loophole
I'll keep escaping eternally

You lost me within the depths
Thinking by you I was found
But I'll never really escape
For by these scars I'm forever bound.

Hourglass

This world is the hourglass
And you are the sand
Pouring all over me
On my cursed land

For all the broken bones
You've always been the cure
You're the love left lurking long
Standing there, proud and pure

You twisted everything around
Only you know how to stop time
For forever lies in your hand now
And forever will you be mine

At least that's what I thought
That's what you made me think
Your sand has filled up my lungs now
I feel heavy like I could sink

But now you've gotten ahold of my hours
And I don't think you're ever going to let go
You made a minute feel like forever
And it's like you want me to know

To know that I'm in your control
Every door you broke through
I'm ten feet deep in your sand
Head to toe, I am covered in you.

Fireheart

Here comes along something
No one has ever seen
Something more complicated than those
Intricate machines

It's a heart with a core so rare
One made of fire
One betrayed by many
Even then it's known as the ultimate liar

It has been walking on the burned pavement
For maybe quite a little too long
That the fire burned its way into the core
And the rhythm of the flame now part of the
song

So fireheart, fireheart
Coming in your way
Bringing ashes to midnight
And the embers to day.

Heart's reigns

In this pandemonium called my head
There is a string of my emotions and people constantly pull it
Retreating deeper into my shell
Rather than dodging each and every bullet

Because I think I have no energy
To stop all of this pain
Chaos is all that's ever caused
Whenever I let someone in my heart's terrain

It used to be covered with soldiers
But someone let down my guard
For now it roams around freely
In my heart's yard

These shrapnels of the wall
Somehow still cover the floor
Even when you're truly gone
You left me yearning for more

Everytime I think of you
My conscience receives a kick
I'd think maybe I was dying
But as usual, it didn't stick

But your spirit has taken over my soul
Constantly flogging it with a cane
And I have no idea where it's going
How can I when you're the one with the control
over my reigns.

Palm of my hand

Among these familiar people
Feels a little out of place
This laughter and this chatter
Blinding within this haze

I'm lost in another world
Unaware of a single thing being said
My attention has dissolved
Drowning in this wine of red

These views and these sights
Have melted away with my interest
Just want to go back home
Find some peace, get some rest

But nobody ever listens
Nobody understands
That I'm counting the seconds till I go
On the very palm of my hand.

The choke

I think this was a mistake
I should have made a note
But rather I chose to tuck it away
In the pockets of my coat

Threw a dream away
A token I never wanted to keep
For always I wanted to blend in
Never be the black sheep

The jokes are a little bit distant
But something I could have known
My head still stares at a blank canvas
Even though I have grown

I feel like the tide
Is going to somehow call out
But I'm actually thinking of jumping in
For maybe it could chase away my drought

My land is all but barren
No life upon it left
All I want to do is steal a happy ending
I don't care if I'm charged of theft

For some comfort I yearn
Among these thousand shadows

My roots used to go so deep
But all my dreams have turned so shallow

I feel a little insufficient
Every step of the way
I've been stepping on the ashes of my wings
All night and day

Maybe this whole thing is an illusion
This whole thing is a joke
And I should escape as fast as I can
Before I got lured into the choke.

Eternal Illusion

Thank god you vanished
Thank god you ran away
Because if you never did
I think I would still stay

And be stuck in an eternal illusion
For my heart you have already broken through
I wish the ground would swallow you up
Or are you now going to cheat death too?

Ghouls

Whenever I look in the mirror
I can see the spirits and ghouls
Doing nothing, just staring
Peering deep into our souls

It can bring out the beast in you
Or it can give you a jump scare
Rather, it decides to just observe you with intent
Doing nothing, just standing there.

Set the world on fire

I don't want to see another guitar
Play it for me, pick it up
I didn't want to be suspended in darkness
And now I think I'm stuck

I don't want to be lured into the ocean
Jump into the sea
I don't want these wings to be clipped
Don't ever set them free

I don't want to hear another sound
Tell me one last lie
I don't want to drift in the clouds
Take me up so high

Your arms were my home
I'm homesick
I didn't want death to be this slow
It wasn't painless nor was it quick

I don't want to get an electric shock
I'm walking on a wire
I don't want to see flame ever again
Set the world on fire.

Glass jars

Your eyes are blind
When you look at my scars
Each moment
I had collected in these glass jars

But glass is fragile
Especially when it's within your range
For you it's all I lie
For you it just seems strange

I'm running out of the good moments
Just like I'm running out of love
I fell into your cage
With just a single shove

This glass jar, it weighs me down
Heavy on my shoulder
Hoping the second you see it
You won't shatter it with your boulder

The tragic creation on my skin
Done by none other than you
My heart bleeding red
But skin black and blue

Your shadow is my demon
Constantly picking silence when I want to scream

The only thing I wish for is
I will one day wake up from this dream

This future that still lies in your hands
A future you're yet to lose
But with each bruise on my skin
Even my heart started to bruise.

Shows

This story, it ended
It ceased to exist
Yet I still hold on to every last memory
Within my fist

It's like time has changed its principles
I'm stuck in the same moment on repeat
A show playing again and again
And I'm forced not to move from my seat

But all I want to do is
Exit this theater
And the movie might still be there
But I'll figure out how to delete it later

I remember everything
Every excruciating hour
But time has scared me into being silent
And so behind these curtains I cower

I have lost my sense of what's real
And what is only a part of the show
Those who drowned in the scenes
And those who are actually trapped in the constant flow

This show can always cease to exist
This show can be dead

This show has stopped playing in front of me
That doesn't mean it will stop playing in my
head.

Lonesome sparrow

I'm locked in a cage without the key found
Yet again have I become a lonesome sparrow
Being set free is the least of my worries
Because I keep getting close to the same arrow

These cruel creatures, they want me dead
And for what reason, I don't understand
Fear tags along everywhere I go
The sky isn't safe for the others, nor is the land

I'm stuck with no hope of escaping
My family from me was ripped
Now I'm the only one in the cage
My wings now trapped and clipped

Look there, I think someone is coming
No one ever comes here
Will they be the reason I perish
I want them to disappear

I flap my wings, out of breath
Hoping they'll get scared and go
But I should've known, I'm just a sparrow
For no fear does this person show

Wait, is that a key in their hand
It seems to look like it

The person puts it in the lock
And turns out, it's the right fit

I fly out of it in an instant
Forever grateful
I start for the forest
For towards it I feel a strange pull

Oh god, there are too many birds here
I just want to be left alone
Why can't I find a place I fit
Where I can be on my own

But I think I said things too fast
I got hunted down by the same huntsmen
In the same cage, wings clipped
A sparrow with no hope to escape again.

Bullet

Bullet, what is wrong with you
Why don't you ever hit
Exactly where I want you to
The Bull's eye on the target

Why do you always float off into space
I had given you a goal
But you never seem to satisfy
Rather you plunged down deep into a whole

Everything is right in front of you
What more do you even want
All the ghosts have left the house
And your future they are coming to haunt

Bullet, what is wrong with you
My expectations have gone low
Bullet, what is wrong with you
Why don't you try to shoot off and go?

Pick up the phone

Hello? Someone please answer
I'm down here all alone
Hello? Someone please answer
Someone pick up the phone

I don't care who it is
I just want someone who'll understand
My lungs, they've forgotten how to breathe
And I'm trying my best not to drag my heart across the sand

Hello? Someone please answer
A helpless feeling overtakes me whenever I click dial
Hello? Someone please answer
Do you want to make me run one last mile

I don't care who it is
I just want someone who will hear me out
I don't care if you're the rain
I just want someone who can feel my drought

Hello? Someone please answer
I'm down here on my own
Hello? Someone please answer
Someone pick up the phone

I'm sorry

I'm sorry the roses lost their colour
I'm sorry the sky is blue
I'm sorry the pages are on fire
I'm sorry for extending each clue

I'm sorry the ocean is so big
I'm sorry the darkness is my friend
I'm sorry the moonlight doesn't fall upon you
I'm sorry the pages never end

I'm sorry the sunset is a comfort
I'm sorry she was in pain
I'm sorry you didn't seem to care
I'm sorry she drove you insane

I'm sorry the world is so big
I'm sorry you went to the darkside
I'm sorry the grass is green
I'm sorry that she was the one that had to hide

I'm sorry the sun is too bright
I'm sorry about her heart's theft
I'm sorry lightning struck your family
But i'm not sorry that she left.

Sayonara

Here I am wondering when will you say
Sayonara
But it will be goodbye for good
Because I could never match up to the person
you wanted
I should've known I never will and never would

I'm wondering when will you say Sayonara
But you'll say it for the very last time
And whatever we have would have shattered
Like the broken glass of a bottle of wine

Adios, I'm sorry you gave up on me
Maybe in another lifetime it'll be.

Ragdoll

I'm the pawn in your game
You can always push aside
You're the very reason
A part of me has died

I'm shaking and shaking
All I want to do is run
But each thought of you is more frustrating
Because even after everything, for you I'd still steal the sun

Something in my head
Keeps banging on a bell
Telling me to forget about you
Trying to convince me I'm alive and well

I'm something you look at for a while
Then you lose your interest
To me, you mean the world
But to you, I'm just a pest

I can't go near you
For I won't be able to trust myself
It still hurts too much
For I'm just a ragdoll on your shelf.

Lightning

Lightning has struck my heart
I'm still trying to recover
Did my best to get over the past
But sometimes around it, I still hover

To my brain it was an awakening
But to my system it was shock
Locked out of some room
Trying my best to pick the lock

The electricity left me disorientated
Maybe that's why I'm not thinking straight
Now I'm trying to break through, kicking and banging
It is still not opening, I'm starting to think it's fate

I can only peek through the keyhole
I honestly don't see much
Can't even make sense of what little I can see
To me it's all Greek, Latin and Dutch

Maybe I should give up for now
In a few years, come back again
When my heart has finally healed from the shock
What happens next, we'll see then.

I saw you in the dark

I'm running around your circus
Because to you I'm just a clown
Pretending day and night that I'm whole
When inside I'm breaking down

Why do all the doors seem to be closed
Everyone seems to go on with life
But the truth is, the world has shattered us all
Licking our blood off a knife

The intelligent hide behind the curtains
The unsure try to walk with reason and be proud
The wounded cover up their scars
But me? I'm still looking for you in every crowd

The memories have turned to ash
The pages are all torn
I had looked for you in the dark
I saw you, I could have sworn.

Sink

When it comes to us everything is lopsided
And so is everything I try not to feel
It's all so simple and at the same time
complicated
Sometimes makes me question if this is real

We used to be in a ship of chaos
So together we jumped into the sea
We swam and swam so far away
Now that ship is all but an insignificant bee

Because I have you to hold onto
In case the ocean is hungry
And if the people find out we are missing
We'll swim far away from the country

You started to give up, go deep into the waters
I didn't let go, instead I too went inside
The beauty I see down is like none other
Like a roller coaster but the best kind of ride

I can't seem to label what this is
I didn't even get enough time to think
I feel so alive and free
Now I'm in too deep but at the same time trying
not to sink

The only reason I haven't gone up to take in some air
Is because you're in the water too
And honestly I don't care if my lungs close up and I drop down to the surface
For in these depths I would sink for you.

One day

If these songs were a language
I would be so fluent
If I were the pages
By you, I would be torn and ruined

If this guitar was a person
It would hold my hand
If wounds could claim a person
It would be bold written on my skin like a brand

If words were a gun
I would get shot and shot
If torture was a spy
I would get caught

If the sky was raining fire
I would have burned away
If your voice was a song
I would forever have it on play.

All lies

You left a scar on my skin
And on my heart
Like the autumn leaves it falls
I can hear it breaking apart

Maybe it will heal
Maybe it will not
The pain might get worse
Within seconds it already feels like I've been shot

The lanterns, I see them
As my love for you dies
You said you would take care of me
All lies, all lies, all lies.

Someone once said

You say I want to go the circus
But I just want to close my eyes
You say wake up early in the morning
But I have no interest in the sunrise

You say take some rest at night
But that's when I feel the most awake
You say I have to try harder, this isn't enough
When I just want to take a break

You say don't let the ground swallow you
But I'm already deep within
You say to go touch the end of the skies
But now that is just another thing to add to my
list of what I could've been

You say to play something in front of people
But I just want to close the door and sing
You say go out and socialise
But that's not my kind of thing

You say the ghosts will keep you up at night
But I have come to love horror
You say the demons always like to be in the
spotlight
So why do I see them hiding in the corner

You say light will always shine upon each being
Then why am I wandering in the dark
You say the flame's core can seep into anyone's soul
Then how come I haven't yet seen a single spark
You say I'll go to heaven
But I have already been through hell
You say you know me
Then I guess you just don't know me that well.

The painting

There used to be a painting
Hung high on a wall
It whispered stories of some sort
Echoing down in the hall

No one could understand the meaning
To decipher it, no one could manage
It seemed to speak out something none could
understand
It's words muttered in some dead language

A man once came in front of it
Declared he could explain what it meant
He thought he did his best
He thought he knew about the artist's hours
spent

But only the creator
Can know the language it speaks
Only they shall know
The secrets it keeps

So old man give up
This code you shall never figure
The secrets hidden behind are too old
And each year they grow bigger

Old man, this isn't something you can ponder about
While looking out the window at the heavy rain
Because after all how can you call this art
When it is something you can explain?

Love is war

Love is war
And turns out I have lost
Little did I know
That my heart would be the cost

I should have known
This was a gone case
But now the only thing I see
Is the look on your face

Whatever I felt, I tucked it in a box
And kept it there for quite a while
These feelings, they go long back
Longer than the Nile

I'm stuck in the beehive
But by you, I've already gotten stung
Somehow, you've taught me how to breathe
with the pain
Without using a single lung

You watched my hands in shock
As I dropped the dagger to the floor
Because you have cast me under your spell
And slowly it seeps into my heart's core

Love is war
I thought this would be easy
But I should have known
Because that very love destroyed me.

Traffic lights

I'm stuck in front of a traffic light
It doesn't seem to hit green
Ahead of the traffic light
Is something no one has ever seen

I've been waiting for quite a while
But the colour is stuck on load
I just want to see what exactly is ahead
But for long, I've been on the same road

I think the system might be broken
I start my way back home
Because breaking the rules is considered a crime
And I can't cross the traffic alone

Now I look back, I feel a bit regret
Everyone had said, only by the rules should you
abide
But now I wonder night and day
What was on the other side

So my advice for you is
It doesn't matter what the rules have said
For if you really want to go but the light never
shows green
You might as well run on red.

Somethings better left unsaid

I have a sister
Whose dreams I don't know
Whose journey will be without me
On the pathways she chooses to go

She has eyes
That won't turn to me
For a reassurance
That she will be set free

She has small hands
Hands I'll never hold
I won't be the person
She'll go to when she's cold

She has legs
That I'll never see dance
When she feels happy
I'll never get the chance

She has a life
One without me in it
A lantern she'll breathe fire into
One I'll never see lit

She will face sorrow
And I won't be there

To show her that there's hope
To show her that I care

I have a sister
Someone I'll never know
But my heart refuses to lose her
It refuses to let her go.

Insane

The hall is empty
The music is playing
Sinking into the rhythm
As my body starts swaying
You call me fool
For dancing so free
Insane for feeling
Everything around me
You don't know that my heartbeat
And the music's beat are forever in sync
And nothing can destroy the connection
Nothing can break the link
You call me dramatic
You call me insane
But how does it matter
When you yourself can't hear the music anyway?

All wrong

The walls are talking for once
But I want peace
The fabric of reality is one bumpy ride
But I'm allergic to each crease

Pain goes away over time they say
But I can hear it screaming in my ears
Don't change, remain the way you are
But everyone has changed, even me in a span of
years

Don't let your fears get in the way
But it's like a shadow, always coming back when
I finally see light
Everyone says if you turn left, you'll end up in a
ditch
But I can't seem to swerve right

Love is a precious thing
But I've ordered my heart to never feel
Sinking out of reality is dangerous
But nothing around me looks real

Words mean no harm at all
Then how come their blade is so sharp
You're safe under the angel's music
Then why am I playing the devil's harp

Go into the forest, and feel everything around you
But I can only hear screeching, no birdsong
They all say something but I can't seem to meet their expectations
Maybe I'm just doing it all wrong.

Other than me

I was the vast ocean
But you never wanted the sea
I was the rulebreaker
But you wanted something risk-free

I was the foggy night
But you wanted the early morning sunrise
I was the complicated monarch
But you wanted a queen in disguise

I was the blue orchids
But you wanted dark red roses
I was the acid rain
But you only wanted poison in small doses

I was the hourglass
You wanted a clock
I was the key
You wanted a lock

I was cranberry wine
You wanted champagne
I was fragile and could get rusted
But you wanted something you could maintain

I was the rings of Saturn
But you wanted to run to Mars

I was the crescent Moon
But you wanted something whole like the stars

I was the hive
But you didn't want to get stung by a bee
I was looking at you
But you were looking at anything other than me.

The town of peace

When reality takes you on a ride
The carriage is bound to come to a halt
And leave you in a town
Where sugar is never supposed to look like salt

I could've stayed inside the carriage
But the town looked so pretty
And I just wanted to feel the countryside air
Since I was tired of the hustle of the city

They all looked at peace
But little did I know
That earthquakes were raging within them too
And this was all for show

Everyone smiled
But the smiles were all fake
That's when I realised
Coming to this town was a mistake

It was better to think
That somewhere in this world was peace
And the people didn't constantly worry
And by every passing hour their faith would not
decrease

But that town only exists
In books and in dreams
For people aren't always
The way they always seem.

When will the world stop turning?

When the world will stop turning
The trees will stop burning
The waters in the ocean will stop churning
Thoughts will stop being concerning
Emotions wanted at bay would stop returning
People will start being a little more discerning
Maybe then for you, I'll stop yearning.

Dead meadows arc

I'd wasted my stardust and moonlight
Thinking that you were in the dark
When all this time I could've been under the sun
But you put me in the dead meadow's arc

The flowers there were wilted
Not a single healthy tree is in sight
Even when all decayed around because of you
I can still only picture you as my knight

The forest berries were poison
The animals ran away
The rivers all dried up
But the barren land stayed

And now I'm trapped inside
They ask who put me in here
It's a man who lured me in
And then soon did disappear

Both my body and soul
You've left a permanent mark
I'd wasted my stardust and moonlight
Thinking that you were in the dark.

Candlelight

Billions of flowers in the garden
But for you, I've chosen to become a rose
Billions of lakes out there
But our love like a river, rapidly flows

Billions of melodies that seem to echo
But only your tune I have in mind
Billions of destinies out there
But somehow ours became intertwined

Billions of frozen hearts out there
But it was mine that you chose
Billions of secrets that have been thrown in my head
All of which, only one person knows

Billions of gems buried in the ground
But only for eternal love am I looking in the mine
Billions of steps in the castle to take
But I want you to only climb up the grapevine

Billions of words come to my mind
But only words about you can I seem to write
Billions of stars are out there
But I crave only for your candlelight.

Stumble

I was walking down the sidewalk
And I tripped and fell into a drain
But even when my senses got knocked out
Everything around was driving me insane
The birds called out to me
Telling me that it's okay
But that's the last thing you might want to hear
When you're about to break into two like a
fragile vase made of clay
So maybe sometimes the only thing you need
When both, body and soul, you're trying not to
crumble
Is a random stranger to pass you by
And tell you that it's okay to stumble.

Flashback

Back then
I heard your name
I smiled
I saw your eyes
I felt something I haven't felt in a while
I heard your voice
My heart ran a mile
Now
I heard your name
I didn't smile anymore
I saw your eyes
I heard the slamming door
I heard your voice
My heart grew sore.

Same page

Take a step ahead
Open a different page
My mind's starting to feel more like a chaotic circus
And my heart more like a cage

But I don't want to go on
I want to be stuck here
Everyone says that it's over, you should feel joy
But I feel anything but cheer

So here I go again, stopping time
Because I don't know what else to do
For if I flip a single page
The next chapters won't have you.

Grapevine

Gather some strength
To climb up the grapevine
Into this dark, empty, hollow
Heart of mine
Softly knock on the windows
Just a few times
And I swear I'll let you into
This dark, empty, hollow heart of mine.

Dove of Death

The skies have blinded you
Hopeful dove of death
Your future is inevitable
They won't stop till your dying breath

They believed in slaughter
You believed in love
And that was the flaw that needed fixing
You stupid hopeful dove

They believed in cruelty
You believed in second chances
They believed in firmness
You believed in letting loose and the rain dances

Go hide behind the clouds
But she's always doing the opposite
And one day, she'll fall from the skies
Into an unforgiving pit

They won't stop looking
They crave blood and feather
If you think this is what being a prey feels like
Trust me, it's not going to get any better

Fly away, stupid hopeful bird
They're hunting you with an unforgiving knife
Fly away, dove of death
Before it costs you your life.

When the movie ends

Maybe one day, when the movie ends
You won't be there in the credits
Maybe one day, when anger is thrown into the sea
I won't be screaming, trying to get it

Maybe one day, when the clouds will rain fire
I'll just dance
Maybe one day, when the walls stop speaking
I'll give people a second chance

Maybe one day, I'll choose my own colour palette
Instead of you keeping on colouring me blue
Maybe one day, I'll be suffocated by smoke
Instead of getting suffocated by you.

Fury

My emotions, going up and down
On a trampoline
In a kingdom called my mind
Fury is the queen

Everyone else just follows
Whatever are the orders
For only fury is allowed to break the rules
Only fury shall cross the borders

She is a tyrant
But also the most powerful of them all
Reluctantly but nevertheless
They always answer her call

She'll destroy the lands
Never mindful of the consequences
When she causes destruction
I'm left mending the fallen walls and broken fences

She fills my head with fog
Leaving me unsure
Her words will wound everything around
And I'm left searching for the cure

And here I am wondering
When will the ruler cease
For now when fury rules
I crave silence and peace.

Christmas girl

You said she was like Christmas
The stockings, the lights, the candy canes
I guess you didn't know her well enough
Because she is clearly, hot chocolate and horror movies on rainy days

You said she was the simple path
But she's the crooked zig-zagged lanes
You said you bled love into her heart
Then why does she feel pain flowing through her veins?

The creature in disguise

Pain might be dead
But in pages pain is alive
The roses might have wilted
But its thorns still thrive

And so a hidden creature
Who was in disguise
Used a pen as its weapon
The camera was its eyes

It crossed the lands
And the seven seas
And went on to write
Uncountable destinies

For a human being is mortal
A writer is not
They have seen the broken hearts
And the wars that were fought

Because they hold power
Wielded by no ordinary man
For even the gods cannot keep something alive
The way a writer can.

Changing seasons

The starting of spring
I looked at the flowers
And my heart too started to bloom
Within just a few hours

Then summer came
My love grew warm
Then rain poured down
Those feelings withstanding the storm

Then with autumn
I started falling like the leaves
Deeper and deeper
Love began to weave

And when winter arrived
So did the costly price
For I was deceived
Now my heart covered in all but ice

And so spring came yet again
A little bit of love shall remain
But after the changing seasons
My heart shan't be the same.

Hit by a train

We stood on the tracks
I heard the the whistle of the train
So I told you to steer clear
While my life went down the drain

So caught up in saving you
And convincing you to flee
That it was only once the train hit
Was that I realised instead I should've saved me.

Caged

The waters of the sea
Forever have raged
And so the monsters down deep
Are growing tired of being caged

For they hold grudges of their own
A rivalry that runs deep
And now that their hunger
Is slowly beginning to creep

The deathless tsunamis
Slowly but steadily begin
And the monsters are stirring
Growing restless within

And when they shall unleash
They'll cause nothing but obliteration
An anger more complicated
Than even the greatest mathematical equation

And so to those who caused the tsunamis
Those who have never been confronted
I warn you, these monstrous creatures will
unleash
And then forever, you shall be hunted.

The rare

The rare, they let their waters churn
And step over knives with utter grace
They catch the others without caring if they fall
If meddled with, they'll punch you in the face

The rare, they don't let the others tame their fire
They live so wild and free
They never get sidetracked
And stay grounded like a tree

The rare, they don't fear the dark
They never tiptoe around the truth
The rare, no matter how old
Have never lost their youth

The rare, only ever focus on what really matters
They can take control of the noise
They speak when the world grows silent
Unlike you, they have a voice.

Pluto was a planet too

They removed you from their minds
They removed you from the chart
They didn't care for the fact
That you were with them from the start

Mercury, was the furnace
And so it became the fever beast
Venus, where the sun rises in the west
And sets in the east

Earth then comes about
Where life grew uncontrolled
Then comes Mars
Just looks warm but really cold

Then the soul of Jupiter
The biggest one, most forget
Then the rings of Saturn
With the most moons yet

Uranus, the seventh one
Where one year there is about 84 Earth years
Then the very last is Neptune
Where crying there transforms into frozen tears

And so only the neglected remember
What others have forgotten, they knew

It was the fact that though all eight have a
purpose
But Pluto was a planet too.

Stubborn Seas

There came a day
When the seas swept over the land
And the waters marked the surface
Like a permanent brand

And so all the foolish
Will blame the stubborn sea
They'll blame us for the dismantled buildings
And every fallen tree

But the waters aren't stupid
Every tide bears a reason and purpose
And we only seek vengeance
When something gets triggered on the surface

But people have grown blind
They'll never discover what was really true
For I was merely just the tsunami
But the earthquake was you.

Printed by Libri Plureos GmbH in Hamburg,
Germany